Look What Came From

Egypt

by
Miles Harvey

Franklin Watts

A Division of Scholastic Inc.

New York Toronto London Auckland Sydney

Mexico City New Delhi Hong Kong

Danbury, Connecticut

Series Concept: Shari Joffe
Design: Steve Marton

Library of Congress Cataloging-in-Publication Data

Harvey, Miles.
    Look what came from Egypt / by Miles Harvey.
        p. cm. — (Look what came from)
    Includes bibliographical references (p.   ) and index.
    Summary: Describes many familiar inventions, foods,
customs, tools, toys and games, fashions, and more that
originated in Egypt.
    ISBN 0-531-11498-8 (lib. bdg.)   0-531-15937-X (pbk.)
    1. Egypt—Civilization—To 332 B.C.—Juvenile literature.
    2. Civilization—Egyptian influences—Juvenile literature.
    [1. Egypt—Civilization—To 332 B.C. 2. Civilization—Egyptian
influences.] I. Title. II. Series.
    DT61.H26   1998
    932—dc21   97-30825
                                                    CIP
                                                    AC

Photo credits © : Ancient Art & Architecture Collection Ltd.: 8 left; The Ancient
Egypt Picture Library: front cover top, 13 right, 23 right, 24 right; Animals,
Animals: 20 top right (Gerard Lacz); Art Resource: front cover bottom right,
14 bottom, 19 bottom right , 20 bottom right, 21 bottom (Erich Lessing), 9, 25
right (Scala/Art Resource, NY); Ben Klaffke: back cover stamp, 4 middle, 4 right,
17 right, 22 right, 25 top left, 25 middle left, 26, 27; Bolton Picture Library:
19 bottom left; The Bridgeman Art Library International Ltd., London/New York:
front cover left, 6 left (Egyptian mummy of a Priestess, 21st Dynasty, 1085-935
BC, British Museum, London), border on pages 4 and 6-32 (Adoration of the
Rising Sun in the Form of the Falcon Re-Harakhty, Egyptian, 20th Dynasty, c. 1150
BC [papyrus], British Museum, London), 7 (Passage from the Second to the Third
Gallery in the Great Pyramid, plate 5 from 'Views in Egypt,' engraved by Thomas
Milton (1743-1827) pub. by Robert Bowyer (1758-1834) 1802 [aquatint] by Luigi
Mayer [fl. 1776-1802] [after] Private Collection/The Stapleton Collection),
20 bottom middle (Several statuettes of the cat-goddess Bast and cat figurines
representing the same goddess, Egyptian, Late Period, c.664-300 BC [bronze],
Bonhams, London); British Museum Photographs: 3 bottom, 12 left, 12 top right,
18 left, 18 right; Charise Mericle: 5; Christie's Images: 1, 19 top, 20 left; C M
Dixon: 3 right, 6 right, 13 left; Corbis-Bettmann: 4 left, 22 left; Envision:
14 top (Amy Reichman); E. T. Archive: 10 bottom; Nik Wheeler: 10 top, 16 right;
Panos Pictures: 12 middle (Jeremy Horner), 16 left (J. H. Morris); Photo
Researchers: 32 left (George Holton); Rengin Altay: 32 right; SuperStock: 11
right (A. K. G., Berlin/SuperStock), 24 left (British Museum, London/ET Archive,
London/SuperStock); Tony Stone Images: front cover background (Joel Simon),
21 top (Jack Daniels); Werner Forman Archive: 15 (E. Strouhal), 8 right (Private
Collection, London), 11 left (Egyptian Museum, Cairo), 23 left

Contents

Greetings from Egypt!

Ancient Egyptians began the custom of shaking hands.

Egypt is one of the world's most fascinating countries. Located in the northeast corner of Africa, it is home to more than 58 million people.

Egypt is a very old land. It was once home to one of the most important civilizations in the world. This civilization is known as ancient Egypt. The history of ancient Egypt began more than 5,000 years ago and came to an end about 2,600 years ago.

Ancient Egypt is often remembered for its fantastic buildings, including the pyramids. Kings and queens were buried in these huge structures after they died. Many of the pyramids are still standing today. Each year, millions of people travel to Egypt to see them.

But you don't have to go all the way to Africa to find out about Egypt. Many things in your everyday life originally came from this great land. The Egyptians even invented the very first book! So let's turn the pages of this one—and find out about all the amazing things that come from Egypt!

The flag of Egypt

Egyptian money

4

Inventions

Have you ever seen a mummy in a horror movie? The original mummies came from ancient Egypt, but they weren't monsters. They were dead people whose bodies were preserved for burial. The process of preserving dead bodies is called **embalming**. The ancient Egyptians invented embalming about 5,000 years ago. Many dead people are still embalmed today, but they aren't wrapped in cloth like mummies were.

Ancient Egyptian mummy inside its wooden case

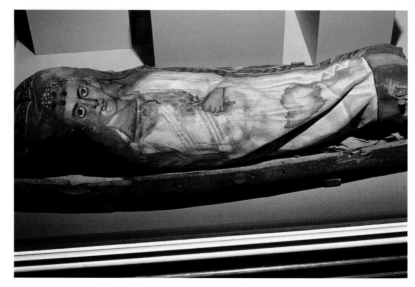

Ancient Egyptian child mummy

Embalming is just one of the many important inventions that come from Egypt. About 5,000 years ago, for example, people in Egypt came up with the idea for **tunnels**. Today, we use tunnels mainly in highways and subways. The ancient Egyptians, however, used them to create huge underground chambers where they buried dead people. Some of these tunnels can be found in the pyramids.

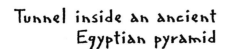

Tunnel inside an ancient Egyptian pyramid

more inventions

People have been using **pens** for about 5,000 years. The first pens came from ancient Egypt, but they were different than the ones we have today. They were made out of the stems of plants. Around the same period that they invented pens, the Egyptians also made the first **ink**. TheEgyptians made the world's first **books** about 4,800 years ago.

Egyptian papyrus scroll

Ancient Egyptian pens and inkwell

But the pages weren't made out of paper. They were made out of papyrus, a kind of plant. These first books are known as scrolls. To read them, you wouldn't turn any pages. You would unroll them, like you would do with paper towels.

Ancient Egyptian wall carving showing people writing with pens

...even more inventions

More than 5,000 years ago, people in Egypt began building boats that had sails on them. With the help of the wind, these sails allowed the boats to move very fast. Many people believe that the first **sailboats** came from Egypt.

A felucca, a type of sailboat that has been used in Egypt for hundreds of years

Painting of an ancient Egyptian sailboat

Ancient Egyptian policeman using a baboon to help catch a thief

The ancient Egyptians were the first people in history to come up with a **police force**. The police officers who lived 4,500 years ago had pretty much the same job that today's officers do—keeping people safe and chasing criminals.

A **lighthouse** is a type of tower built on the seashore. At the top of this tower is a bright light. Sailors at sea watch for this light to make sure they don't crash into the shore. The world's first lighthouse was built near the city of Alexandria, Egypt, about 2,270 years ago. It was 350 feet (107 m) high and its light could be seen from 30 miles (48 km) out at sea!

Fashion

A lot of the things we wear on our bodies and faces were invented in ancient Egypt. For example, the first people to wear **makeup** around their eyes lived in Egypt about 6,000 years ago. Both men and women wore eye makeup. Egyptian women were especially fond of wearing green eye shadow.

Eye-makeup container from ancient Egypt

Some makeup was very glittery. That's because it was made out of crushed beetles and their shiny shells! About 6,000 years ago, the Egyptians were the first people to manufacture **pins**. They used these pins to hold together different parts of their clothing. They also used pins to hold their hair up. Today, our clothes are usually stitched together with thread. But people still use pins as part of their hair styles.

A mask of King Tutankhamen that shows how eye makeup was used in ancient Egypt

This painting of an Egyptian goddess shows a hairstyle popular among the ancient Egyptians.

The ancient Egyptians came up with the idea of wearing **wigs** about 5,000 years ago. Wigs were worn by both women and men. Some of these wigs were very heavy. One Egyptian queen's wig weighed so much that she couldn't walk unless people helped her!

Some people wear **gloves** strictly for the sake of fashion. The ancient Egyptians came up with this idea about 3,500 years ago. In fact, some handsome gloves were found in the tomb of a famous king named Tutankhamen.

Gloves found in the tomb of Tutankhamen

Food

Modern-day pancakes

People have been eating **pancakes** for about 4,600 years. The first cooks to make this delicious meal lived in ancient Egypt. Around the same time they invented pancakes, the Egyptians also discovered how to add yeast to dough to make **raised bread.** But they found that when they cooked this bread over an open flame, the wind made the dough go flat. So they invented the first **ovens:** hollow, cone-shaped containers made of clay.

These bread loaves, found in an ancient Egyptian tomb, are 3,400 years old!

Ancient Egyptian bakers mixing and kneading dough

Modern-day bread seller in Cairo, Egypt

more

food

Women baking bread in a traditional Egyptian oven

The Egyptians made the world's first **candy** about 3,000 years ago. It was made with honey, fruit, nuts, and herbs. The ancient Egyptians did not use sugar or chocolate in their candy, because they did not know these foods existed.

Egyptian candy made with honey and nuts

Toys and Games

Nobody knows exactly when the first ball was invented. But many people think that the first **ball games** came from Egypt about 5,000 years ago. Today, we use balls in many popular games, including baseball, basketball, football, and soccer.

Many other fun games and toys also come from Egypt. Do you like **marbles?**

It is thought that the first children to play with marbles lived in ancient Egypt about 5,000 years ago. And do you like **checkers?**

Ancient Egyptian toy balls

Ancient Egyptian marbles

18

Ancient Egyptians playing a game similar to checkers

The ancient Egyptians invented this fun game about 4,000 years ago.

A board game found in the tomb of an ancient Egyptian king

Babies love to make noise with **rattles.** People in Egypt invented this toy about 3,300 years ago. The first rattles were made of clay and shaped like birds, pigs, and bears.

Ancient Egyptian rattle

19

Animals

We get our love of **cats** from the ancient Egyptians. Not only did they keep cats as pets, but they also considered them sacred. When something is sacred, it is very respected, and is sometimes even worshipped in religious ceremonies.

Mummified ancient Egyptian cat

Today, the kind of cat most similar to those once owned by ancient Egyptians is the **Egyptian Mau.**

Egyptian Mau

Ancient Egyptian cat sculptures

The **greyhound** is a breed of dog that began in ancient Egypt. Dogs that look just like greyhounds can be found in Egyptian artwork that is 4,900 years old!

Modern-day greyhound

Artwork showing ancient Egyptian dog

Ancient Egyptians collecting
honey from beehives

Modern-day beekeeper

More than 4,400 years ago, the Egyptians became the first people to raise their own **bees.** They did this to get honey for various foods and medicines.

Egyptian kings kept big collections of animals from other countries. Some people consider these collections the world's first **zoos.** One king who lived about 3,400 years ago had many large animals, including a rhinoceros, an elephant, and a bear.

Ancient Egyptian wall painting showing exotic animals being brought to Egypt

Egyptian wall painting showing a man with a pigeon

About 3,100 years ago, Egyptians trained pigeons to deliver messages from one place to another. This type of **airmail** came long before the invention of the airplane!

Musical Instruments

The **flute** is a popular instrument that is often used in classical music. People have been playing flutes for about 5,500 years. The original flutes came from Egypt and other nearby lands.

Ancient Egyptian flutes

Wall painting showing ancient Egyptian flute player

24

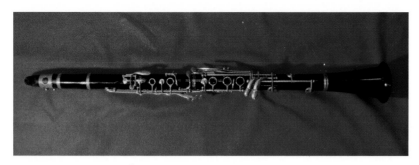

Modern-day clarinet

Modern-day oboe

The Egyptians also came up with the basic ideas for a lot of the other cool musical instruments we still use today. More than 4,700 years ago, the Egyptians invented an instrument called the **clarinet.** Today, the clarinet is used in many different kinds of music, including jazz and classical.

The ancient Egyptians also came up with the basic idea for the **oboe.** The first oboes were made about 3,500 years ago. They were made from cane, the slender woody stem of a plant. Today, oboes are made out of other kinds of materials. But the instrument is still very popular.

Have you ever heard anyone play a **trumpet?** This great-sounding instrument is made of metal and is used in many different kinds of music, including jazz and rock.

Ancient Egyptian trumpet

The Egyptians invented the trumpet more than 3,350 years ago. Some trumpets were found in the tomb of King Tutankhamen.

A Recipe from Egypt

What do you like to eat for breakfast? Cereal? Waffles? Eggs? Bagels? People in Egypt like to eat a breakfast called *ful medames* (pronounced fool meh-DAH-mes). This meal is made from a vegetable called the fava bean, and it's a lot different from traditional American breakfast foods. But try it— you might just love it! You can cook ful medames yourself, with the help of an adult.

Ful medames

To start, you'll need the following ingredients:

1 16-ounce can of cooked fava beans
1 large tomato
1 large onion
1½ tablespoons of olive oil
1 teaspoon cumin powder
1 small bunch of parsley
2 lemons
1 package of pita bread

You'll also need the following equipment:

- a cutting knife (to be used only with adult supervision)
- a cutting board
- a medium-sized cooking pot
- a cooking spoon

You can do the following part of the recipe by yourself, with an adult watching.

1. Wash your hands.

2. Making sure to keep your fingers out of the way of the blade, cut the onion into small squares. This kind of cutting is called chopping.

3. Cut the leaves of the parsley until you have 1/4 cup of chopped parsley.

4. Cut the tomato into tiny squares—even smaller than the onion and parsley. This kind of cutting is called dicing.

5. Cut the lemons in half, and squeeze the juice into a small bowl.

You'll need an adult to do the next part of the recipe, but you can help out by reading the instructions out loud.

1. Pour the beans into a pot and bring them to a boil.

2. Mix the beans well and add the chopped tomato, chopped parsley, diced onion, olive oil, cumin, and lemon juice. You can also add salt and pepper.

3. Bring the mixture to a boil again, then reduce the heat to medium and cook for about 5 minutes.

4. While you're waiting for the ful medames to finish, warm up the pita bread in the oven or microwave.

5. Serve the ful medames with the bread. Now you're ready to eat an Egyptian-style breakfast!

How do you say....?

People in Egypt speak a language called Arabic, which is also the official language in 22 other countries. Arabic uses a completely different alphabet than English does. Try saying some words in Arabic for yourself!

English	Arabic	How to pronounce it
hello	السلام عليكم	ess sa-laam ah-LEE-koom
goodbye	مع السلامة	ma as sa-lahm-a
bee	نحلة	Nahh-la
boat	مركب	MAHR-kib
bread	خبز	eysh
cat	قط	otta
dog	كلب	kalb
papyrus	ورق البردى	war-a el BAHR-jdee
pen	قلم	alam
pigeon	حمام	ham-aam
pyramid	هرم (اهرام)	HAHR-am

To find out more

Here are some other resources to help you learn more about Egypt:

Books

Bickman, Connie. **Egypt.** Abdo & Daughters Publishing, 1996.

Crosher, Judith. **Ancient Egypt.** Viking, 1993.

Defrates, Joanna. **What Do We Know About the Egyptians?** Peter Bedrick Books, 1991.

Grant, Neil. **The Egyptians.** Oxford University Press, 1996.

Terzi, Marinella. **The Land of the Pharaohs.** Children's Press, 1992.

Thomson, Ruth. **The Egyptians.** Children's Press, 1995.

Organizations and Online Sites

Egyptian Cultural and Educational Bureau
1303 New Hampshire Ave., N.W. Washington, DC 20036
http://www.eceb-usa.org

The Little Horus Web Site
http://www.horus.ics.org.eg /
This site is designed to help kids learn about Egypt.

The History of Egypt
http://touregypt.net/kids/History.htm
The official internet site of the Egyptian Ministry of Tourism has a special web page to help kids find out about Egyptian history.

Rosetta Stone
http://www.clemusart.com/archive /
pharaoh/rosetta/
Sponsored by the Cleveland Museum of Art, this site introduces kids to the world of Egyptology and archaeology.

Guardian's Egypt
http://guardians.net/egypt
This web site has all sorts of good information on Egypt—and great graphics. In one part of the site, you can tour different pyramids on your computer.

Odyssey in Egypt
http://www.website1.com/odyssey /
This cool site allows students to watch an archaeological dig in Egypt as it happens.

Egypt map
http://www.lib.utexas.edu/maps/africa/
egypt.gif
Check out this online map of Egypt, provided by the University of Texas at Austin.

Glossary

cane the slender, woody stem of certain plants

civilization the way of life of a people

exotic belonging to another part of the world; foreign

greyhound a breed of dog that began in ancient Egypt

lighthouse a tower, located on the seashore, that is used to guide ships or warn them of rocks or similar dangers

mummies bodies of dead people preserved for burial

papyrus a tall, grasslike plant used by the ancient Egyptians to make paper

pyramids huge, triangular-shaped buildings in which the ancient Egyptians buried dead rulers

sacred having to do with religion or religious use; deserving honor or respect

scroll a roll of paper, especially one with writing on it

tomb a place for the burial of the dead

traditional handed down from generation to generation

Index

Look what (doesn't) come from Egypt!

Egypt is famous for its camels. But the kind of camel that can be found in Egypt has only one hump. Two-humped camels come from the continent of Asia.

Meet the Author

Miles Harvey is the author of several books for young people. He lives in Chicago. This book is dedicated to his mummy-in-law, Camille.